IT'S FUN TO LEARN ABOUT
MY BODY

Arianne Holden
Consultant: Fiona Wyeth

ARMADILLO

NOTES

This book helps children to understand their body and the way it works. Informative text, lively photographs and plenty of fun activities and experiments ensure that children learn in the best way of all – by doing.

Reading together

Children benefit from adult help when reading a book. Do not expect your child to grasp all the information at once! Look at one concept at a time, and allow a few days for the information to be absorbed before moving on to a new topic.

Talking it through

Talk about the things you have found out together. Make everyday activities an adventure in learning. Meal times provide a perfect opportunity to talk about teeth, taste, tongues and healthy food, while an outdoor play session is a stimulus for discussion about what the body can do.

Answering questions

Ask your child questions and encourage him or her to answer. Do not worry if the answers are wrong – making mistakes is part of the learning process. The most important thing is that your child has the confidence to answer. Remember to praise all your child's attempts.

Checking your child's understanding

You can check your child's understanding of how the body works by asking questions like – Why do we get tired? Why is it that we take exercise?

Learning by doing

Encourage your child to try the activities. They have been specially devised to be easy and fun to do. They will also help your child understand that it really is fun to learn!

CONTENTS

Look in a mirror. Do you look like any of these children?

Your body

Everyone is different. You are the only person who looks exactly like you.

head

This is the front of my body ...

... and this is the back.

shoulder

arm

neck

hand

Your body has lots of different parts. All the parts have special names.

waist

hip

thigh

knee

leg

foot

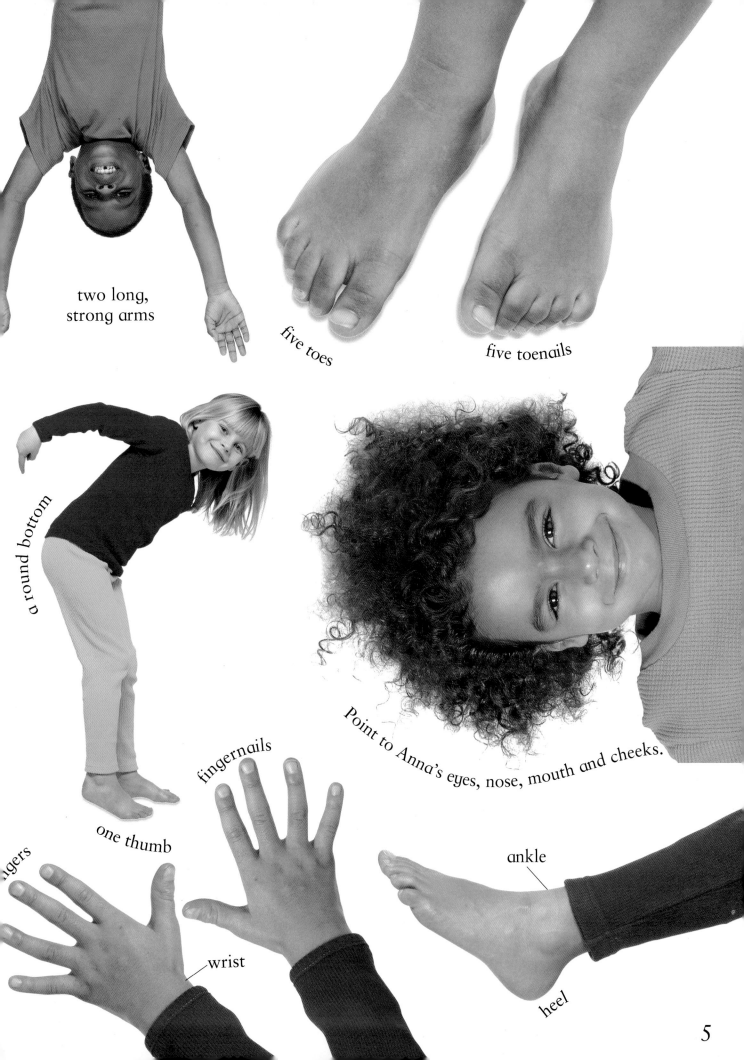

two long,
strong arms

five toes

five toenails

a round bottom

fingernails

Point to Anna's eyes, nose, mouth and cheeks.

ankle

one thumb

...gers

wrist

heel

5

Bones

Inside your body are your bones. Without them, you would be like a wibbly, wobbly jelly.

That is what I look like inside.

There are lots of small bones in your hands.

Bones fit together to make your skeleton.

When you cross your legs ...

... your bones look like this.

When you lie down ...

... your bones look like this.

You can feel hard bones in your ...

... knees

... skull

... elbow

6

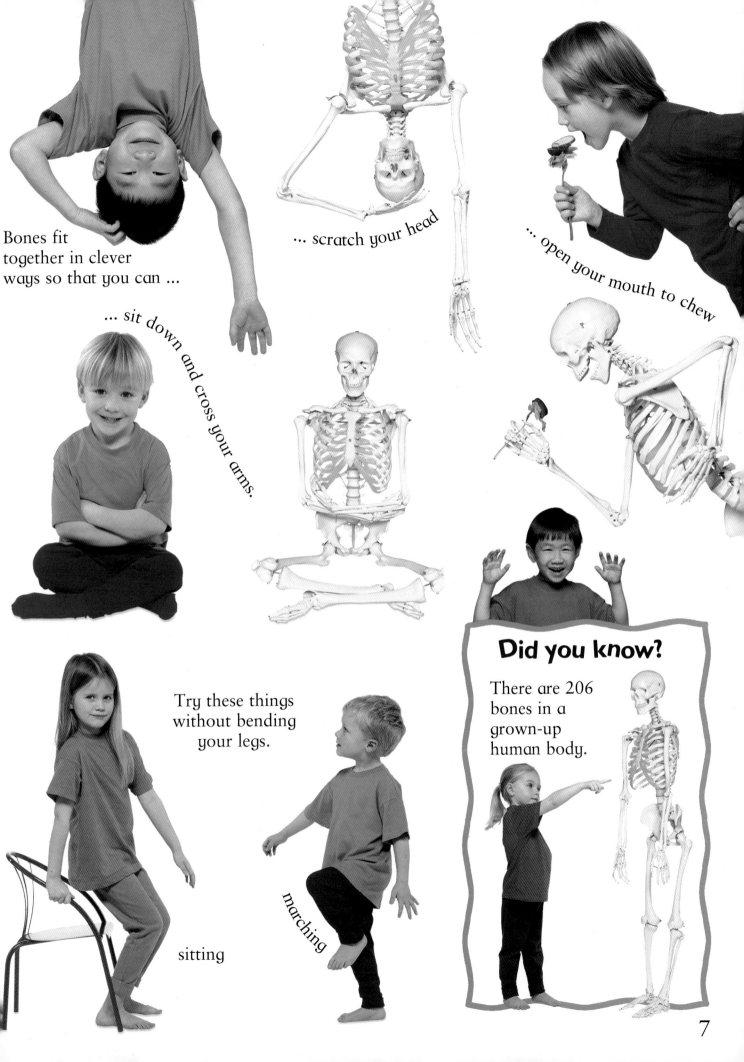

Bones fit together in clever ways so that you can ...

... scratch your head

... open your mouth to chew

... sit down and cross your arms.

Try these things without bending your legs.

sitting

marching

Did you know?

There are 206 bones in a grown-up human body.

7

Muscles

Your body uses strong muscles to help you do amazing things. Your muscles are under your skin.

Strong muscles help you to lift things.

hoop spinning

Bendy, stretchy muscles let you move about.

acrobatics

leaping

jogging

You use muscles in your face to make a ...

... cheeky face

... balloon face

... fishy face

... monster face

Lungs

When you breathe, air goes into your lungs. You need air to live.

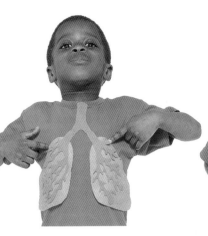

This is what your lungs look like.

Feel yourself breathing.

Your lungs...

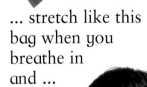

... stretch like this bag when you breathe in and ...

... shrink when you breathe out.

Heart

Your heart is a muscle. It pumps blood around your body.

This is what your heart looks like.

Try this!

See your breath

Stand close to a mirror and breathe on it. Your warm breath will mist the mirror.

Have you ever ... ...cut yourself...

You can listen to a heart beating.

thump ... thump

You can feel blood moving through your wrist.

...or had a nose bleed?

9

Skin

Your skin protects your
body and keeps your
insides inside!

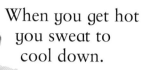

When you get hot
you sweat to
cool down.

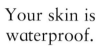

Do you get
goosebumps
when you
are cold?

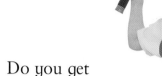

Your skin is
waterproof.

You should
protect your skin
from the sun.

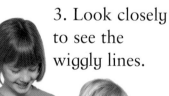

Your skin is soft and stretchy.

Your skin is
covered with tiny
hairs. The hair helps
you to stay warm.

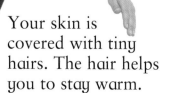

Try this!
Fingerprinting

1. Draw on your
fingertips with
a felt-tip pen.

2. Press them
on to a piece
of paper.

3. Look closely
to see the
wiggly lines.

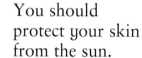
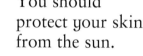

Growing

You are growing all the time. You even grow when you are asleep!

Babies grow into ... young children ... older children ... and then into adults.

Try this!

Make a height chart

Stand in front of a piece of paper stuck to a wall. Ask a friend to mark your height. Wait a month before your height is marked again. Have you grown?

fingernails

Fingernails and toenails grow all the time.

My hair grows longer every day ...

... but I like mine short!

toenails

Eat up!

Your body needs healthy food and drink to keep it working.

I eat lots of healthy food!

Your body needs lots of fruit and vegetables.

Potatoes ... bread ... pasta ... rice ...

... will give your body energy.

Did you know?

You need 7 cups of water every day. Some of this water comes from the food you eat.

fish

nuts

eggs and milk

cheese

Your body needs these foods to make it strong.

beans

seafood

These foods are yummy, but don't eat too many of them.

Teeth

You have hard teeth inside your mouth.
They chew food so that it can be swallowed.

Front teeth cut and slice.

Back teeth squash and grind your food.

Babies have just a few teeth so ...

... they can only eat mushy food.

You can eat all sorts of food.

Brush your teeth to keep them clean and shining.

Try this!

Toothy impressions

1. Ask a grown-up to cut a slice of cheese or apple.

2. Take a big bite out of the cheese or apple.

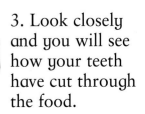

3. Look closely and you will see how your teeth have cut through the food.

13

Taste and tongues

Your tongue is a muscle that helps you to taste your food. This is called your sense of taste.

There are tiny bumps on your tongue ...

... called taste buds.

Can you feel your taste buds?

I love strawberry pudding ...

... but I don't!

Taste buds tell you if food tastes nice or nasty.

Everybody likes different tastes. Do you like to eat...

... spicy hot-dog?

... creamy sweet cake?

... juicy grapes?

14

Would you like to eat these foods?

purple pasta

blue carrots

red bread

blue mashed potato

green fish fingers

blue fries

silver peas

Try this!

Taste and tell game

1. Put some of these foods on a plate. Your friend must not see the food.

salty cracker

sweet, juicy apple

crisp lettuce

tasty cheese

spicy sausage

creamy yogurt

2. Blindfold your friend. Feed them each a different food.

3. Can they name each food?

Can you do these things with your tongue ...

... roll it?

... touch your nose?

... lick your chin?

Smell and noses

Your nose tells you what something smells like. This is called your sense of smell.

Have you ever smelled a flower?

Tiny hairs in your nose help you to smell things.

Do these things smell nice or nasty?

talcum powder

lunchbox leftovers

sweaty shoes

smelly socks

rotten egg

hot chocolate drink

Try this!

Taste test

1. Half-fill four cups with water.

2. Add cordial to one, lemon juice to another, and a little salt to the next. In the last cup is plain water.

3. Blindfold a friend and get them to pinch their nose closed. Ask them to taste and name each drink.

They won't be able to name the drinks because they can't smell them.

These things can make you sneeze.

dust

dogs

cats

hay

rabbits

guinea pig

pollen from flowers

feathers

When you have a cold, your nose is blocked ...

... and you can't taste anything.

Does anything make you sneeze?

Atishoo!

17

Touch

Your skin helps you to feel the things around you. This is called your sense of touch.

A rabbit's fur feels soft and smooth.

What do you think these things feel like?

silky cloth

furry bear

smooth balloons

prickly pineapple

spiky dinosaur

cold custard

Oh no!

sticky, gloopy slime

cold, sloppy spaghetti

Try this!

Touchy feely game

1. Find 7 things that feel very different. Put them in a bag.

rough bark

feather

sticky lollipop

bath sponge

jam tart

metal dish

cuddly toy

2. Ask a friend to feel what is inside the bag. Can they name the things without peeking?

Some parts of our bodies tickle when they are touched.

Where are you ticklish?

Can you tell what someone looks like by feeling their face?

You can feel if something is warm or cold with your ...

... hands

... lips and tongue ... or feet.

Take care! Never touch hot things – they may burn you.

Hearing and ears

Your ears help you to hear all the sounds around you. This is called your sense of hearing.

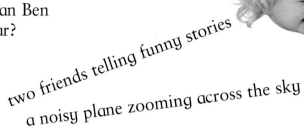

What can Ben hear?

two friends telling funny stories

a noisy plane zooming across the sky

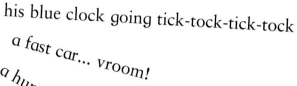

his blue clock going tick-tock-tick-tock

a fast car... vroom!

a hungry kitten miaowing

some loud music

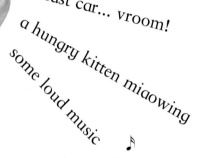

Sound can travel along a string.

You can make sounds **louder** with a megaphone.

Can you hear me now?

What sounds do you make when you ...

... smack your lips? ... blow a raspberry?

20

Have you heard these musical instruments?

trumpet

recorder

saxophone

maraca

tambourine

drum

Some children wear a hearing aid ...

... to help them to hear better.

Try this!

Crazy orchestra

Make funny music by blowing bubbles in a glass of drink, banging bowls and wobbling a sheet of card.

Make some annoying noises.

pop bubble wrap

pop pop pop

grind your teeth

grind grind

eat noisily

crunch crunch crunch

21

Sight and eyes

Your eyes help you to see everything around you. This is called your sense of sight.

Have a look in a mirror. What shade are your eyes?

blue

a pair of beautiful brown eyes

grey

blue-grey

brown

Try doing these things with your eyes closed.

painting

Did you know?

Blind children read books by feeling little bumps on the page. This alphabet is called Braille.

eating

putting on gloves

Glasses help you to see better.

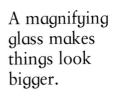

A magnifying glass makes things look bigger.

Swimming goggles will protect your eyes.

Can you see the ten differences in these pictures?

Your eyes can show how you are feeling.

Try this!

Put the tail on the puppy

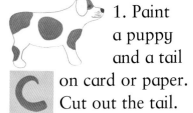

1. Paint a puppy and a tail on card or paper. Cut out the tail.

2. Press sticky putty on to the back of the tail. Fix the puppy to a wall.

3. Blindfold a friend. Spin them three times. Ask them to put the tail on the puppy.

grumpy

cheeky

sad

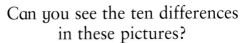

Keeping healthy

You need to look after your body to keep it working well.

You can keep your body fit and healthy by ...

...jumping

Quick, catch the ball!

...swimming

...running

Doing exercise and playing games is great fun!

...stretching

I'm ready!

... playing hula-hoop

Did you know?

When you wash your hands with soap and water, you are washing away germs that could make you very ill.

A bad cough can be caused by germs.

Sue has a cough and now all her friends have coughs.

A handkerchief will stop germs spreading.

flying germs

cough!

cough!

cough!

To be healthy, you have to ...

... get plenty of sleep

... drink water and fruit juice

... and eat healthy food.

If you are ill and have to stay in bed,
a grown-up or a doctor may ...

... give you medicine

... take your temperature

... and ask you to drink water.

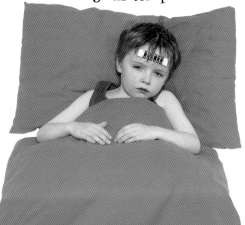

Let's talk

To let others know how we feel or what we need, we talk.

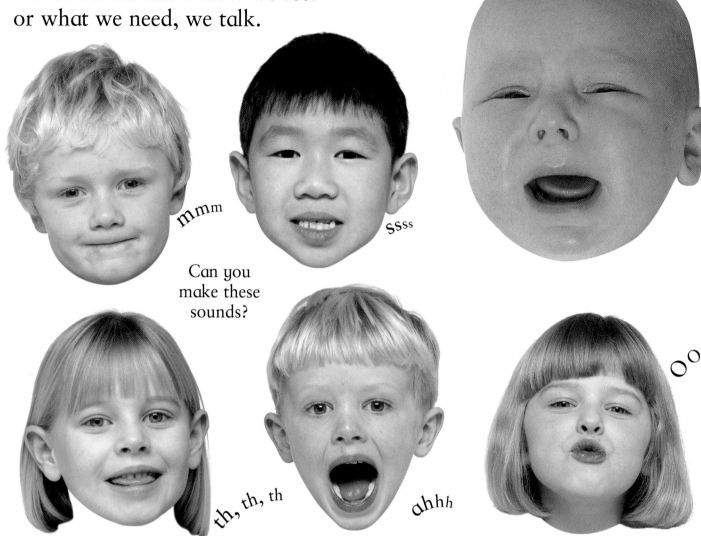

Instead of talking, babies cry.

mmm

ssss

Can you make these sounds?

th, th, th

ahhh

ooo

Place a hand on your throat to feel sounds being made.

Sing 'ooo' and change the shape of your mouth. What happens to the sound?

hello hello hello

ooo

eeee

Sounds can be soft and loud.

quiet whispering

Cover your ears to make loud sounds quiet.

loud shouting

Try this!

Talking with your fingers

Use your fingers to spell out the word 'talk' instead of saying it. This is called finger spelling. It is used by some children who have poor hearing or who are unable to talk.

t   a   l   k

We can talk by making signs with our body.

Do you know what these children are saying?

Brain power

Your brain is in control of everything that your body does. Your brain is working even when you are asleep.

Your brain is inside your head, but you cannot see it.

Your brain is good at thinking. It helps you to...

... build models

... do jigsaws

... read

Here are tricks you can play on your brain. Move your nose towards the two fish.

What happens to the little fish?

Hold a finger in front of your nose and close one eye. Place another finger in line behind it.

Open your eye. Are both fingers in line?

Try this!

A memory game

1. Place ten things from around your home on a plate.

2. Ask a friend to look at them for one minute. Cover the plate.

3. How many things can your friend remember?

You even need your brain to do simple things.

laughing

eating

While asleep you sometimes dream wonderful stories. Have you ever had a dream about ...

... being a famous dancer?

... being chased by a dinosaur?

... being a superhero?

Copy cat game

Roll a die and move counters to see which actions you have to copy. You can play it by yourself or with friends.

counters or buttons

dice

Are yo ready move i actio

1

2

3

Bend down and touch your knees five times.

4

5

6

16

Jump as high as you can.

15

7

Time to get marching.

14

13

10

12

8

9

11

Do five star jumps.

30

20

21

22

23

24

25

Jog once
around the
room.

26

27

19

18

17

Throw and
catch a ball
five times.

28

Close your eyes
and balance
on one leg.

29

30

Hoop-spin or
wiggle your
hips like a
hula dancer.

31

32

33

34

Well done!
Time for a
healthy
drink.

FINISH

This edition is published by Armadillo,
an imprint of Anness Publishing Ltd,
108 Great Russell Street,
London WC1B 3NA;
info@anness.com

www.annesspublishing.com; twitter: @Anness_Books

Anness Publishing has a new picture agency outlet
for images for publishing, promotions or advertising.
Please visit our website www.practicalpictures.com
for more information.

© Anness Publishing Ltd 2015

A CIP catalogue record for this book
is available from the British Library.

Publisher: Joanna Lorenz
Senior Editor: Felicity Forster
Educational Consultant: Fiona Wyeth MA, BEd
Photography: John Freeman
Head Stylist: Melanie Williams
Stylist: Ken Campbell
Designer: Mike Leaman Design Partners
Production Controller: Ben Worley

PUBLISHER'S NOTE
Although the advice and information in this book are
believed to be accurate and true at the time of going to
press, neither the authors nor the publisher can accept any
legal responsibility or liability for any errors or omissions
that may have been made nor for any inaccuracies nor for
any loss, harm or injury that comes about from following
instructions or advice in this book.

Manufacturer: Anness Publishing Ltd,
108 Great Russell Street, London WC1B 3NA, England
For Product Tracking go to: www.annesspublishing.com/tracking
Batch: 7554-23867-1127

ACKNOWLEDGEMENTS
The publisher would like to thank the following children for
appearing in this book: Alice, Ambika, Andrew, April, Ashley, Billy,
Callum, Charlotte, Chilli, Cleo, Daisy, Daniel, Daniel, Eloise, Eve,
Faye, Giuseppe, Harriet, Holly, Irene, Jack, James, Jonathan,
Kadeem, Kari-Ann, Kayla, Kitty, Lana, Lily, Luke, Madison,
Matthew, Milo, Miriam, Olivia, Otis, Philip, Rebekah, Rosanna,
Rubin, Safari, Saffron, Sumaya, Tom, Zaafir, Zamour.

Note – an adult skeleton was used on pages 6–7.